The Magical Coin
By Little SAVERS, Big GOALS

A story from the Little Savers, Big Goals collection

Dedicated to little savers everywhere!

Every Christmas, Santa left surprises for Benjamin.

This year was different, though; whispers of a special present filled the air.

'It's not a present, but it's magic,' his brother Jack hinted.

Whilst laying out milk and cookies for Santa on Christmas Eve, Benjamin noticed a gleaming coin on the windowsill.

It wasn't like any coin he'd ever seen before. It shone bright with its secret message, 'For a Little Saver,' surrounding a sparkling star.

That night, dreams of rubbish trucks and magical coins danced in his head.

Christmas morning arrived, and Benjamin was bursting with excitement. As he unwrapped his presents, he found a beautifully crafted piggy bank with a note that read: 'For a little saver.'

Benjamin remembered the coin from the night before. He fetched the magical coin and gently dropped it into his new piggy bank with a twinkle in his eye.

After returning from his Christmas day walk, Benjamin noticed his piggy bank seemed fuller than he left it.

Upon opening it, he discovered not just the magic coin but many more like it! Beside his piggy bank, there was a note written in glittering ink:

'Dear Benjamin,
The magic coin you found, rewards those who save. It grows and multiplies based on what's already inside.

This is a little taste of the magic of saving and how small amounts can grow over time.

Keep saving, little one, and discover more wonders.

Merry Christmas!
From, Santa'

Benjamin's eyes sparkled. Not only could he now buy his dream rubbish truck toy, but he had also been introduced to a world where saving was its own kind of magic.

Eagerly, he wondered what other financial wonders awaited him on his 'Little Savers, Big Goals' journey...'

FAMILY TIPS

At the end of our magical story, you may be wondering how to bring the magic of saving into your own home. Here are some practical tips to help you and your little saver get started

1. Start Small
   It's never too early to start saving, and it doesn't have to be a big amount. Even saving just a few pennies a day can add up over time and teach your child the value of money.

2. Make it a Habit
   Set aside a specific time each week to discuss finances with your child. Whether it's during a Sunday family lunch or a quick chat before bedtime, consistency is key.

3. Use Visual Aids
   Children love illustrations. Consider using clear jars, labeled for saving, spending, and sharing, so your child can see their money grow over time.

4. Set Goals Together
   Help your child set achievable financial goals. Whether it's buying a new toy, contributing to a family outing, or donating to a charity, having a goal can make the saving process more rewarding.

5 Match Contributions

To encourage saving, consider matching what your child saves. This not only makes the process more exciting but also teaches them the value of employer-matching programs they might encounter later in life.

6 Be a Role Model

Children often mimic their parents' behavior. Be mindful of your own spending and saving habits, as they'll likely influence your child.

7 Introduce the Concept of Interest

You can simulate a bank's interest by adding a small amount to your child's savings at the end of each month. This will teach them about how money can grow over time.

8 Celebrate Milestones

Reached a savings goal? Celebrate it! Acknowledging these accomplishments can make the journey feel rewarding and encourage future saving endeavors.

Conclusion

Remember, the most important thing is to make saving fun and educational. The skills and habits your child develops now will set the stage for a financially secure future. Happy Saving!

Interactive

Interactive Quiz - "What Kind of Saver Are You?"
"Answer these three questions to find out what kind of saver you are!"

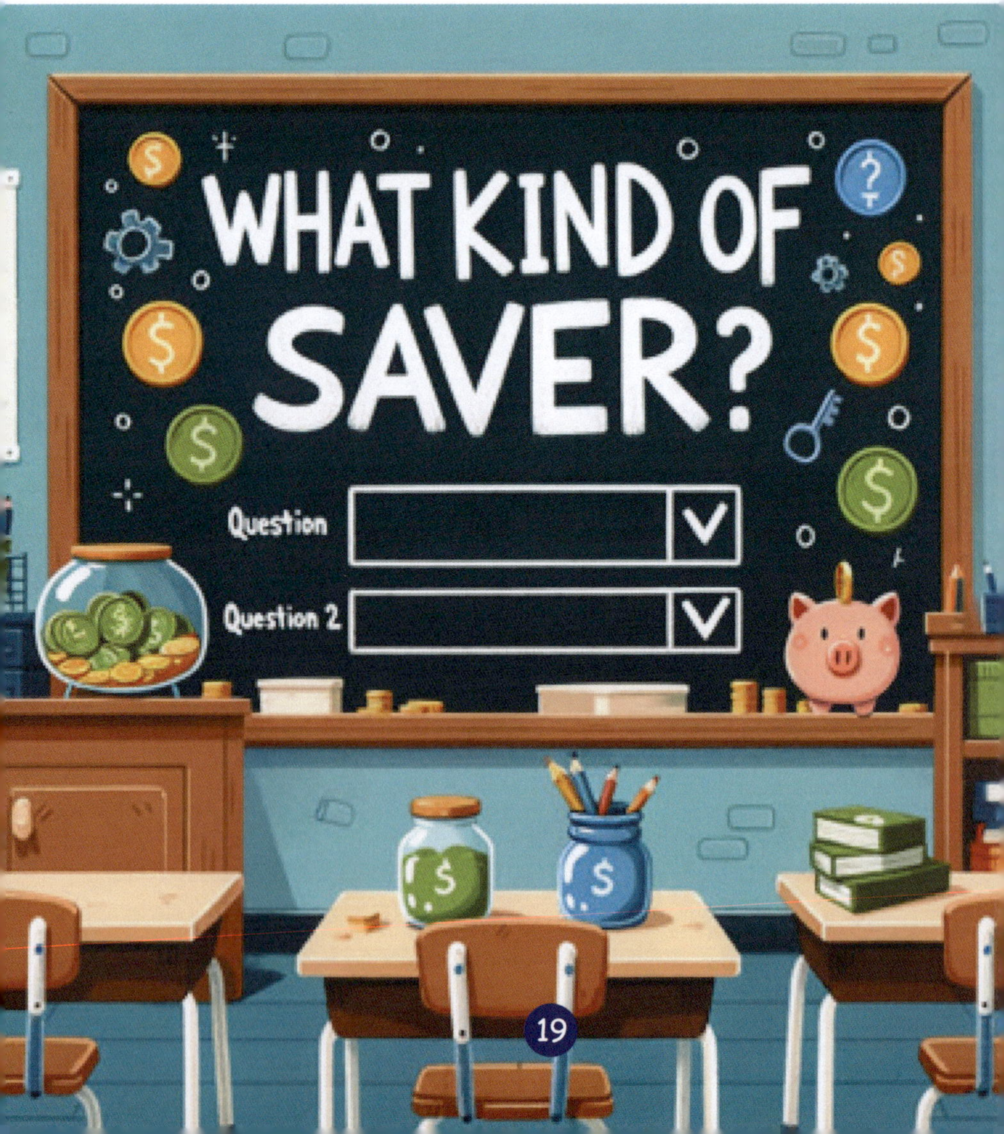

Questions:

Do you prefer to spend your money right away or save it?

A) Save it for something special!
B) Spend some, save some.
C) Spend it! I'll earn more later.

What would you do if you found a magical coin?

A) Save it to help it grow its magic!
B) Use half of its magic and save the other half.
C) Use all its magic at once!

What's your dream purchase?

A) A house or investment for the future.
B) A fun vacation and a small investment.
C) The latest gadget or toy.

Results:

Mostly A's: You're a Super Saver!
You know the value of saving for the future. Keep it up, and you'll reach your big goals!

Mostly B's: You're a Balanced Saver!
You enjoy the present but also save for what's coming. That's a great approach!

Mostly C's: You're a Future Saver!
You love enjoying the moment but don't forget, saving a little can make your future even brighter!

Vocabulary:

Savings: Money that you don't spend right away but keep safe for later.

Interest: Extra money you get or have to give when you save or borrow money.

Budget: A plan that helps you decide how to spend your money wisely.

Investment: Something you buy or spend time on, hoping it will give you more money or benefits in the future.

Goal: Something important you want to do or get, and you work hard to make it happen.

Expense: Money you need to spend on things like food, toys, or going out.

'You've reached the end of our journey for now, but the road to savings is long and rewarding. Keep practicing these tips and playing our games to become a true Little Saver!'

Printed in Great Britain
by Amazon

35457697R00016